Now

Crushing Procrastination and Skyrocketing Productivity

Dan Desmarques

22 Lions

Now: Crushing Procrastination and Skyrocketing Productivity

Written by Dan Desmarques

Contents

Introduction

Are you tired of feeling stuck, overwhelmed, and unproductive? Do you find yourself procrastinating on important tasks only to be haunted by looming deadlines and unmet goals? If so, this book is for you.

"Now: Crushing Procrastination and Skyrocketing Productivity" delves into the complex psychology of procrastination and offers practical, science-based strategies to help you overcome it. Whether you're a student struggling to keep up with assignments, a professional looking to excel in your career, or someone who simply wants to make the most of your time, this book will give you the tools you need to transform your life.

The book debunks common myths about laziness and procrastination, revealing that these labels often oversimplify deeper psychological issues that require a compassionate and holistic approach. By understanding the true nature of motivation and aligning your actions with your deepest values and aspirations, you can unlock a source of energy and drive that will propel you toward your goals.

Throughout the book, the science of motivation, the power of habit formation, and the importance of creating a supportive environment are explored. Practical strategies for immediate action are offered to help you break the cycle of procrastination and achieve lasting success. Whether you're looking to improve your time management skills, cultivate self-discipline, or simply gain a deeper understanding of yourself, this book will serve as your roadmap to a more fulfilling and productive life.

Learn to embrace challenges, overcome self-doubt, and create a life that reflects your authentic self. Don't let procrastination hold you back. Take the first step toward a brighter future today.

Chapter 1: Understanding True Motivation

In our fast-paced society, the terms "lazy" and "procrastinator" are often used to label unproductive behavior. However, these labels are superficial and fail to address the underlying psychological issues. They oversimplify complex issues rooted in our misunderstanding of human motivation.

Contrary to popular belief, motivation is not a finite resource that needs to be constantly replenished. True and lasting motivation comes from aligning our actions with our deepest values and aspirations. When we engage in activities that resonate with our authentic selves, we naturally find the energy and drive to persevere, even in the face of challenges.

Unfortunately, many of us have been conditioned to pursue goals and activities that don't truly align with our inner selves. We've been taught to seek external validation, chase societal ideals of success, and conform to the expectations of others. This disconnect between our actions and our true desires can lead to a profound sense of disillusionment, frustration, and ultimately, procrastination.

In this context, the term "lazy" becomes misleading. Rather than a character flaw or lack of willpower, procrastination is often a coping mechanism. Our minds protect us from facing our limitations, fears, and unmet needs by avoiding tasks. To break out of this cycle, we need to identify and address the underlying issues. This may involve exploring childhood experiences, beliefs, and internalized expectations. It also requires confronting our fears, insecurities, and resistance to change. Through self-discovery, we gain a deeper understanding of our authentic selves.

By aligning our goals and actions with our core values and passions, we can transform productivity from a chore into a joyful journey. And by transforming tasks into engaging experiences with rewards and progress, we can increase motivation and foster a sense of mastery and control over our lives. Approaching our struggles with excitement, kindness, and a willingness to learn can greatly improve our ability to overcome procrastination and lead more fulfilling and productive lives.

Effortless productivity isn't about acquiring more skills or rigid schedules; it's about understanding our motivations and aligning our actions with our true desires. By taking this holistic approach, we can overcome procrastination and unlock personal growth and fulfillment beyond societal expectations.

One of the root causes of procrastination is the belief that we must achieve success through socially accepted patterns. However, success isn't measured by completing tasks or receiving awards and social praise, but by the depth of our self-knowledge and the quality of our lives. Deviating from the expectations or perceptions of others often means feeling successful when others perceive us as failures. On the other hand, many people become demotivated after reaching a certain level of popularity.

Motivation shapes our actions, fuels our ambitions, and ultimately determines the course of our lives, but to truly harness the power of motivation, we must delve deeper into the intricate interplay between autonomy and mastery. Autonomy, the sense of self-determination and control over one's life, is the foundation of motivation. When we feel empowered to make our own choices and chart our own course, a powerful inner drive is ignited.

This autonomy goes beyond mere freedom from external constraints; it includes a deep sense of responsibility for our actions and their results. Conversely, when we feel controlled or manipulated, our motivation wanes and is replaced by resentment and apathy. It is only through self-determination that we move to the next level of our lives, committed to the never-ending quest to become better and to continually improve our skills and abilities.

This innate human desire to excel, to gain competence, and to achieve mastery in our chosen pursuits fuels our passion and sustains our motivation. Mastery is not about perfection; it's about the continuous process of growth and development. It's about accepting challenges, learning from mistakes, and persistently honing our craft. The satisfaction that comes from mastering a skill, overcoming obstacles, and reaching a higher level of competence is immensely rewarding and intrinsically motivating.

In summary, procrastination occurs when our actions don't match what we really want. To overcome it, we must ensure that our goals are aligned with our core values and with what makes us happy.

Chapter 2: The Power of Purpose in Motivation

Purpose is the compass that guides us toward meaningful and impactful endeavors. It provides a clear vision of how our actions contribute to something greater than ourselves, whether it's serving others, creating something beautiful or meaningful, or simply living a life in alignment with our values. Without a sense of purpose, even the most skilled and autonomous individuals can experience a profound sense of emptiness and dissatisfaction.

The interplay of autonomy, mastery, and purpose creates a powerful synergy that transforms ordinary activities into real, lasting achievements. This synergy empowers us to create our own destiny. However, each individual's motivational landscape is unique, shaped by personal experiences, values, and aspirations. To unlock your full potential, it's critical to delve into the intricacies of your own motivational drivers and identify the factors that truly inspire and energize you.

At the heart of this quest is the distinction between intrinsic and extrinsic motivation. Intrinsic motivation, fueled by a genuine passion for the task itself, often leads to higher levels of creativity, persistence, and overall satisfaction. In contrast, extrinsic motivation, driven by external rewards or incentives, can be effective in the short term but lacks the lasting power of intrinsic drives. Beyond this dichotomy, other powerful motivators emerge, such as the pursuit of status and the influence of social proof.

The desire for recognition and validation can be a powerful force, driving individuals to remarkable achievements. But it should be balanced with a strong sense of inner drive to prevent unchecked ambition from taking over. Similarly, the tendency to conform to the behaviors and beliefs of our peers can provide a sense of belonging and validation, but it can also potentially stifle individuality and personal growth.

The pursuit of mastery is closely tied to intrinsic drive. By aligning your goals and actions with your deepest intrinsic drivers and strategically incorporating extrinsic motivators and other influencers, you can create a synergistic ecosystem of motivation that propels you forward with unwavering determination. This is an ongoing process of self-reflection that requires constant adaptation to the ever-changing environments of work, relationships, and personal interests.

In the workplace, for example, staying motivated requires a clear understanding of your values and goals, a focus on the positive impact of your contributions, and a connection with colleagues who share your values. Pursuing professional development opportunities that align with your aspirations facilitates this alignment.

In personal relationships, open communication, mutual respect, and shared goals are essential to maintaining motivation and fostering thriving relationships. When challenges arise, actively seeking solutions while cultivating empathy and understanding is critical to overcoming resentment and maintaining your commitment to the relationship. Understanding human motivation, both in ourselves and in others, is key to achieving lasting success.

Motivation is a complex interplay of psychological and emotional factors that influence our actions and decisions. But when people feel empowered to make choices that align with their values and aspirations, they are more likely to engage in tasks with enthusiasm and persistence. Self-reliance empowers people to take charge of their lives and overcome any challenge that comes their way. Therefore, we must remain vigilant for divergence of purpose and ensure that our values and those of others are aligned toward the same goal.

People who put their own interests ahead of others rarely form successful business partnerships, friendships, or marriages. When we align our purpose with our values and those of others, we tap into a source of determination that sustains us even in the most challenging circumstances. This focus builds resilience, maintains group cohesion, and enables us to overcome setbacks with unwavering commitment.

To achieve this, we should start small, focus on one or two manageable changes at a time, and build on our successes gradually. Remember that motivation, like personal hygiene, requires daily care and consistent effort. We must feed our minds with constructive thoughts and patterns to create a solid foundation for growth and fulfillment. This proactive approach keeps us engaged and focused on our goals. By understanding and nurturing our intrinsic motivations, we can create a life of purpose and satisfaction that transcends the superficial appeal of external rewards.

In summary, understanding what drives us is the key to long-term success. When we act in alignment with our values and goals, we tap into our own inner drive that propels us to accomplish amazing things. This alignment makes us stronger, fosters teamwork, and gives us the courage to persevere in the face of challenges.

Chapter 3: Creating a Supportive Environment for Lasting Motivation

Surrounding yourself with supportive people who challenge you to be your best self is critical. You must learn to distinguish genuine connections from those based on superficiality or envy, because the quality of your relationships has a significant impact on your motivation. Trusting your instincts, which often reveal truths beyond the rational mind, is an important skill that shouldn't be overlooked. They help us adapt to the ever-changing environment of our lives. Adapting to this fluidity allows us to actively shape our motivational landscape rather than simply react to circumstances.

Life is a complex interplay of factors that shape human behavior. These factors, such as the search for meaning, the need for safety, the avoidance of pain, and the pursuit of pleasure, play a central role in human actions and decisions. Recognizing this interplay allows us to align our goals and behaviors with the optimal environment in which they can flourish. When we find meaning in our work, security in our relationships, and opportunities for personal growth, our motivation is at its highest.

When these drivers are out of balance, we can find ourselves stuck in procrastination and a deep sense of disconnection from our true selves. For example, the unwavering commitment to honing skills and pushing boundaries that fuels the drive for mastery can be a powerful motivator, leading to remarkable accomplishments. In the wrong environment, however, such determination can lead to setbacks, resentment, envy, and various attempts by others to sabotage our results.

Similarly, the influence of social proof can be a double-edged sword, providing a sense of belonging and validation, but also running the risk of stifling individuality and limiting personal growth. The key is to cultivate a balanced approach for lasting motivation and fulfillment. But motivation is also about the strategic application of techniques to cultivate it in different life contexts. Without external pressure, we rely on our internal drive to persevere.

When we feel isolated, we need to set clear, achievable goals, break large tasks into smaller, more manageable steps, and celebrate each accomplishment along the way. Regardless of the context, fostering self-motivation often involves overcoming internal obstacles such as self-doubt. But by actively challenging negative self-talk, we can break free of these patterns. Replacing self-criticism with self-compassion and adopting a growth mindset empowers us to persevere in the face of adversity.

By delving deeper into our thoughts, emotions, and behaviors, we can identify the patterns that lead to procrastination and consciously interrupt them. We often become our own harshest critics, berating ourselves for perceived shortcomings and perpetuating a cycle of self-doubt and avoidance. However, by learning to treat ourselves with the same kindness and understanding we would extend to a valued friend, we can break free from this destructive pattern and approach our goals with renewed confidence and determination.

Motivation is a dynamic process that requires constant nurturing and adjustment. To keep moving forward and avoid falling back into procrastination, we need strategies for maintaining motivation, cultivating self-discipline, and embracing flexibility. However, we need to be aware that feelings of being overwhelmed can trigger procrastination. When faced with large or complicated tasks, we may feel intimidated by the sheer size of what needs to be accomplished. This overwhelming feeling can lead to a state of paralysis where we struggle to identify the starting point.

The inability to break tasks down into manageable steps exacerbates feelings of anxiety and inadequacy, further fueling the cycle of procrastination. In addition, attention deficits, whether caused by conditions such as ADHD (Attention Deficit Hyperactivity Disorder) or the constant distractions of our modern world, contribute significantly to procrastination. Individuals with attention deficits often find it difficult to focus on tasks, making it difficult to initiate and complete work. The lure of more immediately gratifying activities, such as scrolling through social media or surfing the web, further complicates our ability to stay on track. But by implementing strategies to address these challenges, we can create an environment that supports sustained motivation and personal growth.

In summary, surrounding ourselves with supportive people and creating a balanced environment are key to staying motivated. Understanding the importance of meaning, security, and enjoyment empowers us to create goals and behaviors that align with our true selves.

Chapter 4:
Holistic Strategies for Increasing Productivity

Practical strategies such as optimizing the work environment, using technology effectively, and applying time management techniques can significantly improve productivity. Creating a focused and distraction-free workspace, setting clear priorities, and using tools such as the Pomodoro Technique can help us stay on task and achieve our goals.

The Pomodoro Technique is a time management method that breaks work into 25-minute intervals followed by short breaks. After four Pomodoros, a longer break is required. These regular breaks help prevent burnout and maintain mental clarity. But it's important to remember that productivity is not just about checking off tasks; it's about living a fulfilling and purposeful life. While external rewards such as financial gain, fear of punishment, or the desire for social approval can be effective in the short term, they often fail to provide the lasting fulfillment and inner drive that intrinsic motivation can cultivate.

In addition, we must learn to recognize and appreciate the moments when adversity can be overcome with joy, and when pain often precedes healing. This understanding allows us to reframe our perspective, embracing the cyclical nature of life and the opportunities for growth that arise from even the most challenging obstacles. Recognizing that inner harmony precedes outer success requires honest self-evaluation and the courage to confront the limiting beliefs that shape our lives.

This approach to life isn't about achieving perfection, but rather finding the courage to challenge our false beliefs and comfort zones. Life is a complex puzzle, and embracing it means finding balance between all the important things. This includes self-control, health, relationships, learning, creativity, fun, and financial stability. This holistic approach to goal setting goes beyond the traditional way of setting goals.

At the heart of it all is self-control, the foundation upon which everything else rests. By learning to control our impulses, emotions, and behaviors, we build discipline and resilience. By setting goals that help us develop self-control, we gain the strength to overcome challenges and temptations that get in our way. But self-control and health are closely related. When we take care of our bodies and minds, we feel better. We need to exercise regularly, eat healthy foods, and do things that help us relax and think clearly. When we take care of ourselves, we're not only stronger and healthier, but also more confident and able to handle whatever life throws at us.

Relationships are equally important, as they have a significant impact on our mental health and happiness. Goals in this area may focus on strengthening existing relationships, developing new meaningful connections, or improving communication skills. Healthy relationships provide emotional support, encouragement, and accountability.

Learning is a lifelong journey that broadens our horizons and fuels our capacity for innovation. Whether it's through formal education, new skills acquired through reading, or self-directed exploration, our goals in this area cultivate an insatiable curiosity and adaptability - essential qualities in an ever-changing world. By continually expanding our knowledge, we open ourselves to new opportunities for personal and professional growth and position ourselves to thrive in the face of evolving challenges. But knowledge alone is not enough to adapt to an ever-changing world. Creativity emerges as a powerful force that enables individuals to generate new ideas and express themselves authentically. To truly excel, people need the right and most up-to-date skills, the ability to analyze different perspectives and think differently, and the courage to acknowledge and accept their emotions. Participating in creative activities not only brings joy, but also strengthens problem-solving skills that benefit us both personally and professionally.

Creativity should not be confused with recreation. Recreational goals revolve around leisure, relaxation, and activities that bring us joy and rejuvenation. intentional time for leisure allows us to recharge our mental and emotional batteries, prevent burnout, and promote a healthier work-life integration. It is worth remembering that the need for self-development, relaxation, and the acquisition of wealth are not separate endeavors, as many believe.

While wealth isn't the only indicator of success, it does provide the financial security and freedom that can facilitate the pursuit of other goals. But it's important that wealth-related goals be aligned with our values and ethics to ensure that financial prosperity doesn't compromise our integrity or well-being.

In summary, true productivity is about living a happy and meaningful life. By focusing on self-control, taking care of your health, nurturing your relationships, learning new things, being creative, finding joy, and being financially stable, you can achieve a holistic sense of self-care.

Chapter 5: Leveraging Mentorship and Time Management for Success

The guidance of mentors can be incredibly valuable. Connecting with peers who can offer encouragement, accountability, and different perspectives can greatly enhance our progress and keep us motivated. They can also help shape our actions. Every action we take reflects our inner beliefs, desires, and priorities, and since everything in life requires investment, the difference in our results can be significant if we wisely allocate our most precious resource: time.

Effective time management goes beyond simply scheduling tasks; it involves consciously prioritizing activities that truly align with our long-term goals. These goals serve as the foundation for building a structured routine that fits seamlessly into our daily lives. Consistency is key, as research shows that it takes an average of 66 days to form a new habit. To create a positive feedback loop that reinforces our progress and builds momentum, we should start small and gradually increase the duration or intensity of our desired behaviors.

Celebrating small victories along the way not only builds our confidence, but also fosters a sense of accomplishment that drives us forward. Rewards solidify the association between a behavior and a positive outcome, increasing the likelihood that the habit will be repeated. Because every action stems from an emotion, we must align our thoughts, feelings, and behaviors to achieve our goals. By cultivating a positive attitude and creating an environment conducive to productive habits, we move closer to our goals.

This positive attitude can be strengthened by believing in our results. The ability to perceive the intangible and believe in our aspirations is an example of the power of belief. In fact, research has shown that an over-reliance on extrinsic rewards can sometimes undermine intrinsic motivation. Individuals may begin to view an activity as a means to an end rather than a source of enjoyment. That's why many wealthy people emphasize that money is not the ultimate goal, as opposed to those who see it as the solution to their problems.

The difference between the wealthy and the less fortunate often lies in their understanding of the source of wealth. The wealthy recognize that wealth comes from a knowledgeable mind, the power of ideas, and the proactive implementation of those ideas by overcoming the fear of failure, while the less fortunate may neglect their need for education in favor of gambling their savings, believing that luck, not intelligence, is the most reliable way to escape their misery. This mindset not only perpetuates financial hardship, but also contributes to a spiritual state of poverty that often affects future generations born into such environments.

In religious contexts, the wealthy often pray for opportunities while the destitute pray for money. But money can be fleeting and often leads to short-term gains, while opportunities for lasting business can provide real financial security. Rather than focusing solely on money, it may be more beneficial for those in need to seek employment and build a stable future. When people unexpectedly receive more money or financial blessings, they often spend it impulsively and end up back where they started. This tendency is related to the fear of wealth.

Effectively changing this mindset requires a profound psychological transformation, including a reevaluation of beliefs about money, increased discipline, increased self-esteem and a sense of responsibility. Research suggests that combining faith with mental imagery can increase self-esteem and a sense of responsibility. A study by Holmes, P. S., & Collins, D. J. (2001) suggests that mental imagery can enhance physical performance by creating a mental blueprint that matches actual experience.

This technique has been used successfully in sport psychology to improve athletic performance. Visualization techniques, which involve mentally rehearsing desired outcomes, can be highly effective in improving performance and achieving goals. In addition, a study by Pham, L. B., & Taylor, S. E. (1999) found that process-based mental simulations, which involve visualizing the steps necessary to achieve a goal, were more effective than outcome-based simulations, which focus only on the desired end result. Effective visualization involves imagining not only the desired outcome, but also the steps and actions necessary to achieve it, thereby increasing the chances of success. This process-based visualization also increases motivation.

In summary, mentoring and effective time management are fundamental to achieving your goals. Maintaining a positive attitude, believing in your goals, and using visualization can really help you stay motivated and achieve success. And by aligning your actions with your core values, you'll be well on your way to building wealth and achieving lasting success.

Chapter 6: Turning Deadlines into Opportunities

The dynamic interplay of anticipation, reinforcement, and challenge creates a motivational landscape that encourages individuals to pursue their goals with unwavering commitment. Visualization techniques play a critical role in overcoming setbacks by creating anticipation and fostering belief in the achievement of desired outcomes despite setbacks and challenges along the way.

Maintaining hope and belief in a specific outcome enables us to perceive the intangible, which is paramount in the face of adversity. When we align our daily activities with a clear sense of purpose, coupled with belief and visualization of our desired outcomes, we tap into an inexhaustible well of inspiration, creativity and determination. By consciously aligning our thoughts, beliefs and actions with these pillars, we break free from procrastination and unleash our true potential.

But only by understanding the underlying drivers of our behavior can we consciously shape our motivations and align them with our deepest aspirations and values. This process involves confronting illusions and embracing personal growth, even when it's challenging and isolating. It also requires recognizing that our limitations are often self-imposed mental constructs. As we expand our knowledge and develop our skills, we must reject environments and people that impede our progress and prevent us from achieving our goals. The notion that we should not share our dreams with others stems from this fundamental truth, although it is wiser to avoid associating with people with whom we cannot share our lives.

This capacity for discernment requires humility, acknowledging our strengths and weaknesses, and actively seeking opportunities to learn, experiment, and challenge ourselves, even in the face of uncertainty or the risk of failure. The most enduring source of motivation is the pursuit of a meaningful life, accompanied by obstacles we can overcome. Yet we often overlook this when we allow people into our lives whom we believe we can change through argument and reason. This approach wastes time and energy explaining.

Purpose transcends the need for acceptance, external approval, or even material wealth. It is a deep understanding that our time on earth is scarce and how we use it contributes to the realization of our personal vision of an ideal future that transcends our physical journey. Cultivating a sense of purpose requires introspection and reflection on our core values, passions, and the legacy we want to leave behind. This includes identifying the causes that resonate with us and envisioning the impact we want to make in the world.

Meaningful relationships based on mutual respect, compassion, and a shared sense of purpose provide the emotional, practical, and intellectual resources we need to overcome procrastination. Seeking and accepting help from others is a sign of strength, not weakness. By acknowledging our limitations and being open to asking for support, we demonstrate a commitment to our own development. This is especially true when it comes to deadlines.

Far from being mere constraints, when used skillfully, deadlines can serve as powerful tools to help us effectively identify the elements of our lives that propel us forward and those that impede our progress. Deadlines create a sense of urgency and focus, helping us to prioritize tasks, improve time management, and mobilize our resources. This heightened state of focus increases our productivity and fosters a deep sense of accomplishment when we achieve our goals.

To effectively harness the power of deadlines, we must actively challenge negative self-talk, visualize desired outcomes, and break large tasks into manageable steps. In doing so, we can transform deadlines from sources of stress into opportunities for achievement and personal growth. Instead of seeing time as a relentless taskmaster, we can learn to use it as a precious resource to fuel our growth, gain a deeper understanding of the true value of our relationships, and manifest our dreams.

In summary, when viewed as opportunities for personal growth and achievement, deadlines can be incredibly powerful tools. By aligning our actions with a clear sense of purpose and an unwavering belief in our abilities, we can overcome procrastination and unleash our full potential. This process involves confronting self-imposed limitations, seeking the support of others, and cultivating meaningful relationships.

Chapter 7: Building Momentum for Success

Sometimes our big aspirations can feel overwhelming and cause us to become stuck in our current situation. Instead of trying to tackle everything at once, breaking down our goals into smaller, more manageable steps can facilitate steady progress and build momentum. Real change comes from the consistent and disciplined execution of seemingly insignificant actions.

Daily habits and routines, such as regular exercise, mindful eating, and meditation, lay the foundation for success in all areas of life. When we focus on short-term goals that can be achieved within days or weeks, these small steps can provide tangible accomplishments and motivation to keep moving forward. Celebrating these victories creates a positive feedback loop that fuels our desire to tackle the next challenge.

Like a boulder rolling downhill, our actions can gain momentum and strength with consistency and purpose. Each completed task and milestone propels us forward, making seemingly insurmountable obstacles to our long-term goals seem more attainable. By aligning our daily habits and short-term goals with our larger, more ambitious aspirations, we create a harmonious balance in various aspects of our lives.

In a professional environment, micro-steps can include setting aside time each day for skill building, networking, or strategic planning. These small actions, when accumulated over time, lead to steady progress toward our career goals, whether it's securing a promotion, launching a new business, or transitioning to a more fulfilling field of work.

In the financial realm, basic steps include budgeting, saving, and managing debt. We can consistently take these small steps to achieve short-term goals, such as increasing income through side hustles or strategic investments. In doing so, we lay the foundation for long-term financial stability and the freedom to pursue our passions without financial constraints.

Similarly, the micro-step approach can be equally transformative for our emotional well-being. By incorporating regular practices of self-reflection, journaling, and stress management into our daily routines, we cultivate emotional resilience. This enables us to navigate the challenges of our personal and professional lives with greater ease.

Intellectual growth is also fueled by a structured approach to goal setting. Rather than mindlessly consuming vast amounts of information, we can cultivate a consistent reading habit by setting achievable goals, such as reading 20 pages a day, actively participating in collaborative learning experiences, and continually seeking opportunities for continuing education and skill enhancement. As these micro-steps accumulate over time, we expand our knowledge and open new avenues for personal and professional growth.

Along the way, the social sphere cannot be overlooked, as our connections with others have a significant impact on our overall well-being and happiness. By setting small, achievable goals related to networking, community involvement, and nurturing our existing relationships, we can gradually build a supportive and enriching social network that positively impacts our lives. The key is to cultivate relationships that resonate with our aspirations and empower us, rather than drain our energy.

For example, I've had numerous conversations with successful entrepreneurs from various nations who have inspired me to produce more and better books. Their perception of my work as a timeless wonder capable of uplifting countless souls has made me feel honored and responsible to produce better work. In contrast, most of the people I've met from various backgrounds have made me feel inadequate for not conforming to their narrow ideas of what a writer, a book, or my lifestyle should be. And while some have praised me for my freedom to travel, many others have tried to convince me that my lifestyle, achieved after a decade of multiple jobs, is wrong.

The negative influence most people had on me was evident in my emotional state. They demotivated me, made me lose interest in my work, and often caused me to procrastinate. In contrast, the group of entrepreneurs I've met have inspired me to look for ways to improve myself and my work. This difference is significant and cannot be ignored. Many people are more interested in seeing us struggle, fail, and give up than they are in seeing us succeed. They get satisfaction from our failures, as evidenced by their smiles at our exhaustion and lack of results. And often, many of these people are our own family members.

In summary, achieving your dreams is all about breaking them down into smaller, more manageable steps. By taking consistent, disciplined actions, such as daily habits and short-term goals, you'll build momentum and make your long-term dreams feel more attainable. Along the way, remember to surround yourself with supportive and positive people who believe in your abilities.

Chapter 8: Facing and Overcoming Resistance

People who want to improve themselves often face resistance from others. Some people are complacent and resent those who have the courage to pursue their dreams. We must keep going and sometimes confront those who try to stop us from achieving our goals. These people may insult us or even become violent if we don't agree with them or if they don't like how we deal with their arrogance, selfishness, and delusional ideas about life.

While meditation and walks in the park can help us regain the energy to cope with stressful environments, they aren't enough to sustain a long-term motivational effect. The people we interact with have a significant impact on our motivation levels over time and can cause us to procrastinate when their energy is low. To remain consistently productive, we need to clearly identify these influences and make an effort to avoid them.

Self-awareness coupled with proactive measures provides the ideal balance between our authentic selves, the energies of the world, and our creative expression. It's in moments of contemplation, reflection and clear thinking that allow us to connect with something beyond ourselves that we can deepen our understanding of our place in the universe. The challenges we face, the lessons we learn, and the connections we make along the way shape us into the individuals we are meant to be. Recognizing how everything affects us also requires an understanding of the complex relationship between our physical environment, our mental state, and our productivity strategies.

A well-designed, distraction-free workspace surrounded by the right people promotes focus, collaboration, and goal achievement. To increase productivity, we need to make our workspace as efficient and focused as possible. This means carefully arranging our furniture and tools so that everything we need is within easy reach. We also want to create a calm and quiet environment, which can be achieved by using noise-canceling headphones, turning off notifications, and creating designated quiet zones. But achieving this ideal work-life balance can be especially challenging for remote workers and independent contractors, who face the unique challenge of separating their work and personal environments.

To maintain focus during work hours, independent workers can set specific work hours, create a dedicated workspace, and communicate their availability to family members or roommates. The use of technology can streamline processes, improve communication, and facilitate collaboration, all of which contribute to increased productivity. Project management software, communication platforms, and automation tools can also help us stay organized, reduce manual data entry, and free up time for strategic activities.

However, it's important to strike a balance when integrating technology into the workplace. Over-reliance on digital tools can lead to information overload and increased distractions. We should regularly evaluate our use of technology to ensure it is aligned with our productivity goals. This may include decluttering digital files, unsubscribing from unnecessary notifications, or setting specific times to check email.

Self-assessment, a powerful self-awareness tool, provides valuable insight into our behavioral patterns and areas for improvement. By establishing consistent patterns with measurable results, we can create an environment conducive to growth and accountability. Understanding the reasons behind our actions is critical to making lasting changes that help us achieve our long-term goals. By recognizing the connection between our actions, thoughts, and emotions, we can shift our focus to actions that move us closer to our goals, rather than getting distracted by the mundane aspects of daily life.

Our productivity isn't just about how much we get done or how efficient we are. It's also about how we handle challenges, learn from our mistakes, and continue to grow. For those who fear failure, viewing mistakes and failures as opportunities to learn and grow can reduce the pressure to be perfect. Self-assessment provides this opportunity because it can be used as a method for self-evaluation and to gain greater awareness of motivational triggers and distracting elements.

In summary, we often encounter resistance when pursuing our dreams, but self-awareness and proactive measures can help overcome these obstacles. To be productive, we need a good workspace, we need to know how to use our technology, and we need to take time to check in with ourselves. Productivity isn't just about being fast, it's about growing and getting better.

Chapter 9:
Breaking Free from Self-Sabotage

Setting realistic expectations and embracing imperfection can greatly reduce anxiety about starting or completing tasks. Self-awareness fosters personal growth, while the illusions we create often lead to regret. When motivation wanes, it's crucial to reconnect with the reasons behind our original goals. Reconnecting with the intrinsic motivations and aspirations that originally inspired us can reignite interest and enthusiasm. Introducing variety and novelty into our routines can also rekindle that spark. Engaging in new activities or changing our approach to existing tasks provides a fresh perspective and renewed motivation.

When these strategies don't work, it's important to recognize that procrastination can stem from psychological factors rooted in past traumas, fears, anxieties, and self-sabotaging behaviors influenced by beliefs or self-image that manifest in our thoughts and actions. Confronting our idealized selves through visualization, such as creating a mental image of our desired accomplishments, allows us to delve deeper into our subconscious and reflect on what is holding us back. This process begins by acknowledging our emotions and allowing them to lead us to their source. Emotions lead us to our memories, where we rediscover forgotten influences on our choices and self-sabotaging behaviors.

For example, a family's strong opposition to our ideas and investments in current endeavors can create a deep-seated fear of rejection. This fear can prevent us from stepping outside our comfort zone or pursuing more ambitious financial goals, even when their opposition no longer has an impact on our lives. Similarly, social rejection in times of abundance can leave us traumatized and fearful of greater wealth because of past experiences of insult and violence. Our fears may not always have a rational basis, but our subconscious doesn't distinguish between real and imagined threats. In fact, the traumas, fears, and anxieties we carry around with us serve as our body's natural defenses to protect us from harm, whether real or imagined.

Fear is an innate survival instinct, and those who lack it often meet unfortunate ends. For example, taking selfies from dangerous heights, riding motorcycles recklessly without a helmet, or driving without regard for others on the road are all examples of people who have disregarded their fear and met death as a result. Fear and anxiety are fundamental aspects of our body and mind that ensure our survival. The body will not prioritize a dream over its own survival. Therefore, it is crucial to confront and neutralize our fears and anxieties as we pursue our aspirations.

It is equally important to consider how our dreams contribute to our survival. Many people struggle financially and fail to achieve their dreams because of conflicting beliefs about survival. For example, while money can improve our lives, many people have a deep-seated belief that accumulating wealth is selfish and will strain friendships, lead to a loss of respect from family members, and even result in rejection by their religious community. As a result, they prioritize social status over financial hardship. Instead of focusing on accumulating wealth, many individuals value having a well-developed social life and feeling respected. These individuals often find solace in keeping a miserable or unsatisfying job, even if they don't openly admit it.

Although deviation from the social norms of one's environment can lead to failure, that failure is usually due to self-sabotage and procrastination rather than misfortune. The truth is, behind every story of someone who failed to build a successful business, there is an individual who prioritized comfort over hard work and neglected their sense of responsibility. Instead, they focused on their social and family image. They did this because they chose the status quo over taking action.

When we claim to have failed, we often deceive ourselves and others about the real reasons for our downfall. This is especially true when we consider that true failure occurs only when we give up. Moreover, before failure, people often seek justification for their results from within and without, either by making themselves sick or by causing others to change their circumstances. People often look for excuses to give up rather than take responsibility for their actions. They want to avoid self-blame and explain their failures to others without feeling accountable. True accountability means accepting that we set ourselves up for failure, and people don't want that because it would force them to take responsibility for their results.

In summary, setting realistic expectations and accepting imperfection can reduce anxiety and increase motivation. To break free from self-sabotaging behaviors, we need to look at the psychological factors behind procrastination. Past traumas and fears can hinder our progress, so it is important to confront and neutralize them.

Chapter 10: Confronting Social Sabotage and Cognitive Dissonance

I t's not uncommon for people to sabotage their own and others' successes in order to convince themselves of their own truth and avoid cognitive dissonance. For example, I remember how certain past relationships negatively affected my writing career. The women I dated believed I was destined to fail, and in order to make this belief congruent with reality, they encouraged me to spend money on extravagant travel and dining out, and often made excuses to disrupt my plans, hindering my ability to achieve my goals.

This pattern extended to my family members, who refused to support me when I decided to pursue a college education after living on the streets. Later, they also refused to help me start a business by denying me the necessary funds to purchase an already successful business. Even friends at the time tried to convince me that my efforts were futile.

As a student, when I got good grades, teachers would invalidate my exam results, claiming that I had to retake the exam because too many students had failed. The real reason was that I had the highest grade and my personality didn't fit their ideal of a successful student. I didn't fit their idea of how a successful citizen should behave or what kind of personality he should have. I also didn't have the background to justify my results.

People try to maintain their idealized view of the world, associated with social status, social hierarchy, and social order, to avoid the discomfort of being wrong about everything they believe to be true. They'd rather sacrifice a black sheep for the sake of all the others than accept uncomfortable views. Throughout my life, I've observed that many people will go to great lengths to ensure our downfall, especially when it comes to religious beliefs.

Religious adherents often argue that wealth and spirituality should not coexist, that working hard is a sign of lack of faith, and that one should rely solely on God. But these ideas are absurd and imply that hard work is inherently wrong. Consequently, they seek to undermine those who challenge these beliefs through their lifestyles, even when these individuals are simply acknowledging and appreciating the divine blessings in their lives that they have prayed for.

Many of these people also tried to stop me from reading various books and writing, claiming that I was doing a disservice to humanity and that the only books worth reading had already been written. Some even suggested that I get a "real" job and dismissed my writings as mere personal opinions because their congregation disagreed with my views. They placed their arrogance above truth, their opinions above my knowledge, and refused to engage in debate because it would force them to admit their own mistakes. And, as I often found, they also disagreed with the views of their own founders and contradicted their own books.

Beyond disagreements among members of a particular religion, we often find ambiguities in very old scriptures, many of which have been mistranslated. This means that we can literally get conflicting interpretations depending on which section of the religious books we choose to analyze and how we interpret the words in those passages. For example, Matthew 6:24 says, "No one can serve two masters. For either you will hate the one and love the other, or you will be devoted to the one and despise the other. You cannot serve both God and money." But Proverbs 10:22 says, "The blessing of the Lord brings wealth without painful toil." And Ecclesiastes 5:19 says, "When God gives someone wealth and possessions and the ability to enjoy them, to accept their lot, and to be happy in their toil-that is a gift from God."

Unfortunately, the vast majority of people refuse to adjust their views of wealth and instead cling to their own interpretations in order to avoid admitting their own mistakes, to avoid shame, and to seek conformity in their relationships and views. As a result, being at odds with a group often means being ostracized. The more I devoted myself to personal growth and improvement, the more I lost friendships and even the respect of family members who began to spread rumors about my supposedly evil nature.

This behavior stems from the fact that when people dislike you, they will resort to slander and defamation, even if they once professed to love you. This behavior may also be related to envy and resentment of their own failures in life.

In summary, people often sabotage the success of others in order to maintain their own beliefs and avoid cognitive dissonance. This behavior can take many forms, such as putting people down or spreading rumors, and it can be fueled by religious beliefs, where people may ignore or even attack those who disagree with them.

Chapter 11: Psychological Biases and Their Effect on Society

Humans are fundamentally emotional creatures who will often disregard everything you've done for them in favor of suppressing their feelings of inadequacy, especially if arrogance is involved. Unfortunately, many people we meet turn against us as soon as we become more successful and achieve what they never did or probably gave up on. They become consumed with feelings of inadequacy, inferiority, and failure.

This phenomenon is not limited to individuals, but extends to groups and nations. Nations often plunder and colonize others for their resources. Instead of looking inward and reflecting on their choices, most people project their negative emotions onto others, blaming them for their feelings as if they were the cause. That's why there is so much hostility when we succeed.

People never acknowledge the hard work, failures, sacrifices, and suffering we endured for our successes. They simply claim that we were lucky while they were unlucky, and that we don't deserve what we have, but they do. Often they also believe that the universe is scarce and limited, and that we've taken what was originally meant for them, or that they should have the same for no particular reason.

Social inequality is a global problem that contributes to crime and violence, as do political ideas that impoverish nations in the name of the common good, such as communism. In countries like the Philippines, where poverty is widespread, lending money often leads to murder by those who can't pay it back. In Brazil, the top 10% hold more than 40% of the national income, while the bottom 50% hold less than 10%, and this inequality is closely linked to Brazil's high homicide rate, which exceeded 40,000 victims in 2023, one of the highest in the world.

Social psychology studies show that people often blame external factors for their failures. This phenomenon, known as self-serving bias, can lead to hostility and resentment toward successful people. For example, research by Miller and Ross (1975) showed that people tend to take credit for their successes but blame external factors for their failures, which can contribute to projecting negative emotions onto others.

In contrast, a 2011 report by the United Nations Office on Drugs and Crime (UNODC) found that safe communities foster a sense of well-being and security, which can lead to higher levels of social cohesion and productivity. People who feel safe are more likely to participate in community activities and contribute to the local economy. In addition, a Harvard Business School study (1999) found that psychological safety in the workplace is associated with increased productivity. Employees who feel safe and supported are more likely to take risks, innovate, and collaborate effectively.

For these reasons, relocation can have a significant impact on our well-being and productivity. When relocation is not an option, a practical way to increase our inner peace is through meditation. Regular meditation practice trains the mind to focus and reduce distractions. A simple meditation involves sitting quietly for a few minutes, focusing on the breath, and gently redirecting the mind when it wanders. This practice not only calms the mind, but also strengthens your ability to focus on tasks. Research has shown that even short daily meditation sessions can lead to improved attention and cognitive flexibility, both of which are critical to productivity.

A study published in Psychiatry Research found that participants who meditated for 10 minutes daily for two weeks experienced significant improvements in attention and working memory. Another study conducted at the University of North Carolina at Charlotte found that even brief sessions of mindfulness meditation can improve cognitive function, including sustained attention and executive function. But another equally effective method for improving mental well-being is mindful observation. This involves taking a moment to stop and observe your surroundings, thoughts, and emotions without judgment.

For example, if you feel the urge to procrastinate, take a few deep breaths and focus on the sensations in your body, the thoughts racing through your mind, and the emotions you're experiencing. This practice can be even more effective outdoors, where you can sit in front of a lake, river, or ocean and feel the breeze on your skin. This practice helps you detach from immediate impulses and make more conscious choices.

In summary, people often project their negative emotions onto successful personalities, blaming them for their own failures and shortcomings. This phenomenon, fueled by self-serving bias and a scarcity mentality, breeds hostility and resentment. Fortunately, practices such as meditation and mindful observation can help individuals increase their well-being and productivity.

Chapter 12: Confronting Imposter Syndrome

Clarity of purpose can greatly reduce feelings of overwhelm and procrastination. For example, instead of setting a vague goal such as "work on the project," you might specify "finish the first draft of the introduction by noon". This specificity provides direction and makes the task feel more manageable. In addition, by taking a closer look at our procrastination triggers, weaknesses, and moments of reduced mental clarity, we can develop effective strategies for overcoming these states. And by identifying specific times of day when we're less productive, we can avoid important tasks during those times and instead engage in easier activities or recreation.

This sense of accountability, coupled with self-assessment, allows us to take proactive measures rather than reactive reactions to procrastination. We shouldn't blame ourselves for our results; instead, we should align ourselves with how our bodies and minds respond. For example, when I arrive in a new country, it may take some time to find the ideal work environment. I don't feel the same energy in every place, and some are undoubtedly more conducive to my productivity than others. While I may feel overwhelmed and exhausted in some places, I may be highly productive and focused in others. But instead of wasting time trying to figure out why, I focus on choosing the right environment.

Many people spend an inordinate amount of time looking for explanations and become frustrated when they don't find them. They believe that everything needs a "why" and a "how" before they take action. As a result, they avoid exploring things they can't explain to others. They equate success with having a plan and find it difficult to imagine life without one. But this mindset creates a predictable path that often leads to failure. A simple shift in focus could lead to greater success.

They resist changing their mindset because it contradicts a fundamental aspect of their personality. Their belief system is intertwined with their decision-making process, and changing their mindset would undermine not only the value of their past decisions, but also their sense of authenticity. This resistance is the root cause of imposter syndrome, a psychological pattern in which individuals doubt their skills, talents, or abilities and fear being exposed as a fraud. Despite evidence of competence, they remain convinced that they don't deserve their achievements, attribute success to luck rather than ability, and fear being exposed as incompetent.

Overcoming imposter syndrome involves changing our thinking patterns, such as rejecting the need for a plan or explanation for our actions. The less you feel the need to justify your decisions, thoughts, and results, the more likely you are to achieve your goals. Explaining things to others shifts your focus from seeking opportunity to seeking approval. This alignment with failure patterns occurs whenever you feel the need to justify your thoughts and decisions to other people.

Successful people often have trouble having normal conversations with those who don't share their mindset. As a result, they may find themselves with fewer friends or alone on their journey to success. People typically avoid the things and people they don't understand or have some control over. Overcoming their challenges requires dismantling self-doubt - an insidious enemy that whispers lies, impedes progress, and paralyzes action - while confronting the limitations of others' understanding and how they use those limitations to convince us that we are wrong and they are right.

Humans are fundamentally self-centered, selfish, and driven by the need for acceptance and comfort. For this reason, they are more likely to rationalize their beliefs and conform to neurological pathways that have been solidified over years than to change. To change would invalidate not only themselves, but everyone who has convinced them that their way of thinking is correct. In fact, they may react violently when confronted with the truth they cannot accept, perceiving it as an affront to their status quo and a threat to their social identity. Their violent outbursts are psychological defense mechanisms designed to protect them from madness because they fear what the truth might reveal about themselves and the people they have trusted.

In summary, understanding the purpose behind our actions and recognizing the triggers that lead to procrastination are key to overcoming self-doubt and achieving success. Imposter syndrome, which stems from the need for constant justification and approval, can keep us from taking risks and embracing new opportunities. To break out of this cycle, we must confront our self-doubt, challenge societal norms, and focus on personal growth rather than seeking external validation.

Chapter 13: Overcoming Self-Doubt Through Introspection and Acceptance

No one reacts more aggressively to the truth than someone who has failed repeatedly. Those who fail often avoid confronting their failures because they trigger overwhelming negative emotions from which they've carefully distanced themselves. These emotions are connected to buried memories of disappointment, betrayal, or abuse. People who have failed too often are overwhelmed by memories they desperately want to repress. They then fabricate an identity around the repression of emotions and memories in order to prioritize social acceptance.

No one presents a greater facade to their true identity than someone who is ashamed of their past. Such individuals fail not because they lack knowledge, but because they are afraid to reveal their true selves to others and to themselves. The truth frightens them because it confronts them with their inadequacies and painful memories. A single trauma can often define a person's entire existence. Once revealed and overcome, however, it can completely change a person's personality and lead him or her in unexpected directions.

Healthy people are often unexpected and unpredictable because they can take responsibility for their choices and accept their past, no matter how shameful or traumatic. Conversely, the most unhealthy people become extremely predictable because of their inability to change and introspect. Those who deny responsibility often can't because they fear the consequences of their past mistakes and traumas. This fear prevents them from confronting their memories and accepting the emotions they evoke, which is necessary to transcend them and embrace their future with absolute responsibility for their personal actions.

Embracing change and overcoming self-doubt requires facing our fears and accepting the past. And while finding the right therapist can accelerate success by enabling us to confront and choose to remember the things we'd rather forget, the therapeutic outcome is irrelevant if there is not already a willingness to take responsibility for our lives by reprogramming our minds and reshaping our relationship with ourselves. The journey into the depths of our subconscious, where our authentic selves are often buried beneath layers of trauma, requires a conscious decision to reprogram our minds and reshape our sense of self.

The first critical step is to identify the source of self-doubt. Self-doubt is not an inherent flaw, but a learned behavior influenced by external pressures and internalized negativity. While the opinions of others can be important, they should not define our self-worth. Social validation, while tempting, is fleeting and unreliable. True self-esteem comes from internal validation-the recognition of our inherent worth and potential. Achieving this requires an unwavering commitment to self-improvement.

Negative self-talk - the constant barrage of critical internal commentary - can be a formidable obstacle that reinforces self-doubt. It's critical to identify and challenge these negative thoughts and replace them with affirmations of strength and ability. This cognitive restructuring is necessary to combat self-doubt because, although our minds are powerful tools, they're easily influenced by negative biases and conditioned patterns. To overcome these, we must cultivate a conscious awareness of our thought processes. A shift in perception reduces anxiety and promotes confidence and clarity.

You can also recall moments of happiness in your life and try to understand why they made you feel that way. You're likely to uncover layers of suffering and frustration that undermined your authentic self, led you down unpredictable paths, and may still be influencing your current perceptions of life and choices. Embracing the unknown in yourself and the world, and accepting the possibility of setbacks in others and yourself, is paramount.

This is the essence of forgiveness. It's not about forgetting, it's about acknowledging the limitations in others and ourselves. The Christian prayer of forgiving others, as we ask God to forgive us, should be interpreted as recognizing the limitations in others, just as we recognize our own imperfections. In fact, the earliest known written record of the Lord's Prayer in Koine Greek, the language of the New Testament, found in the Gospels of Matthew and Luke, suggests that the phrase is more accurately translated as "Forgive us our trespasses as we have forgiven our debtors," which is more in keeping with the concept of imperfection.

In summary, individuals who avoid confronting their failures often do so to suppress negative emotions and memories, creating a false sense of social acceptance. To truly overcome self-doubt, however, we must identify the underlying cause and challenge negative thought patterns. Forgiveness, not as forgetting but as acknowledging imperfection, plays a crucial role in freeing us from self-sabotaging tendencies.

Chapter 14: The Spiritual Importance of Forgiveness

In ancient Greek society, the concept of debt (ὀφειλήματα - opheilēmata) was of immense importance and went beyond mere financial obligations. It encompassed a wide range of moral and social obligations, including those to the gods, family, and community. For example, hospitality (xenia) was a sacred duty, and failure to fulfill it could be considered a moral debt. Similarly, obligations to the gods, such as sacrifices and offerings, were considered debts to be repaid in order to maintain divine favor.

The Lord's Prayer, first written in Koine Greek, illustrates this concept by using the term "ὀφειλήματα" (debts) to include both financial and moral obligations. Here the debt goes beyond mere financial matters; it encompasses our moral and spiritual well-being. This prayer is meant to summon the courage to overcome the failures of others while acknowledging our own shortcomings. It's a way of freeing ourselves from the burdens of the past and the resentments it holds. It serves as a testimony to the power of trauma over our minds and as a practice aimed at reducing the influence of our resentments on our ability to make effective decisions.

To illustrate this concept, Jesus tells the parable of the unforgiving servant in Matthew 18:23-35. In this parable, a servant who is forgiven a large debt refuses to forgive a smaller debt owed to him. This parable encapsulates the principle of forgiveness and the moral obligation to forgive others as we have been forgiven. By asking for forgiveness of debts as we forgive our debtors, the petitioner acknowledges the reciprocal nature of forgiveness and the moral imperative to extend mercy to others. This principle suggests that a lack of forgiveness leads to negative karma in our lives, which can be overcome through the act of forgiving others. By reshaping our views of ourselves and others, we can overcome the limitations of past traumas and cultivate a life of fulfillment and peace.

Moreover, the Christian imperative that our inability to forgive ourselves and others can affect our outcomes holds true from other perspectives as well. Holding on to resentment and a sense of injustice can consume us with anger and lead to actions that jeopardize our future and potential. Research suggests that individuals who dwell on memories of injustice and negative actions by others often have difficulty thinking clearly and making sound decisions (Skolnick et al., 2023). This emotional turmoil can create a cycle in which anger fuels depression, which leads to procrastination (Maynard et al., 2022; Skolnick et al., 2023).

This ancient wisdom holds true when we recognize that it is rooted in the perception that our destiny is intertwined with our greatest karmic challenges. While free will is often associated with the ability to make choices, in a spiritual context it is more accurately understood as the ability to understand and accept divine law. In this context, forgiveness emerges as a critical virtue that precedes acceptance and arises from a deep understanding of the spiritual origins of our suffering. By recognizing how others influence our suffering, we simultaneously gain a heightened awareness of our own contributions.

In addition, when we realize how the people who have had a profound influence on our lives are all connected to our personal desires, we can begin to understand our journey more clearly. For example, my family negatively influenced my self-love, self-esteem, and self-confidence, which hindered my ability to create work that matched my dreams and creativity. Teachers and professors doubted my talents and independence, claiming that I was wrong because I didn't conform to their perspectives. Various psychologists, psychiatrists, and religious figures I've encountered have questioned my moral integrity and intentions because of their negative views of my thought processes. In addition, individuals I've encountered in various countries have questioned the value of my existence through their racism, prejudice, and self-righteousness. They have negatively judged my lifestyle and profession. If I had succumbed to these negative energies, I wouldn't be writing this book or living the life I've always wanted.

Research has shown that external devaluation can significantly influence an individual's self-perception and moral reasoning

(Kaygusuz et al., 2023; Mróz et al., 2024). Other research suggests that experiences of discrimination can lead to feelings of resentment and anger, which can hinder personal growth (DeMarco, 2024; Kaygusuz et al., 2023). In other words, my journey to becoming a writer, although predetermined at birth, was guided by karmic lessons that I had to learn. Ignoring these lessons would have led to increased resentment, suffering, and ultimately, failure to achieve my dreams.

In summary, holding on to resentment and negative experiences can be an obstacle to our personal growth and the realization of our dreams.

Chapter 15: Spiritual Education and Karmic Lessons

Our deepest desires are inextricably linked to our soul's destiny, which explains why the more suffering we endure, the more likely we are to dream of our true destiny. Life offers no other option than to complete a cycle of karma, accompanied by spiritual education through its lessons. Since our existence on earth is fleeting, these lessons may seem clear and repetitive. In my case, for example, I had to learn self-love and self-reliance, and I also had to free myself from the constraints of social norms before I could succeed as a writer.

Our karma is undoubtedly related to mistakes made in past lives, but while we often associate karma with sin and punishment, it's more accurate to think of it as a self-imposed lesson. We create our own karma through our misunderstandings. Therefore, self-forgiveness is essential to breaking the mental chains that bind us to our past experiences. We must transcend the suffering we've endured in order to create a better life in accordance with our aspirations. Without this ability, we fall into self-pity and self-justification, allowing the past to dictate our existence on earth and possibly future reincarnations.

While we can speculate about the causes of loss of self-love, loss of discernment, and fear of ostracism, the higher our potential, the more likely we are to face these challenges. In this way, we recognize that we all face similar challenges at different spiritual levels. For example, for someone at a very low cognitive and spiritual level, writing a book is a challenging task that can feel insurmountable, even for a lifetime, compared to someone at a higher level of consciousness. Thus, comparing oneself to others in this and other matters creates unnecessary obstacles and a sense of inadequacy.

For individuals at a lower spiritual level, preparing a nutritious meal and practicing charity may be more effective in accumulating positive karma. Several religious texts emphasize the importance of charity in gaining God's favor. For example, the Mahabharata states: "Charity given out of duty, without expectation of return, at the proper time and place, and to a worthy person, is considered to be in the mode of goodness." Similarly, Sura Al-Baqarah 2:274 says: "Those who spend their wealth in the way of Allah and do not follow up their gifts with reminders of their generosity or with harm, their reward is with their Lord." Proverbs 19:17 says: "He who is kind to the poor lends to the Lord, and He will reward him for his deeds."

When we encounter people who embody our desired qualities, we may face significant challenges that manifest themselves in their imperfections, either because they harbor envy or simply cannot tolerate anyone with a different perspective. This intolerance stems from their selfish and narcissistic view of themselves. In this context, however, we are reminded of the importance of seeing the shortcomings in others as we see them in ourselves, recognizing that we can discern the good qualities from the imperfections, just as we perfect ourselves despite our own imperfections.

"Forgive us our imperfections as we forgive the imperfections in others" would be an appropriate way to paraphrase the concept of spiritual debt manifested in the original Christian prayer. Another way of saying it would be "Forgive us our spiritual limitations as we acknowledge the spiritual limitations of others," which places us and others on the same spiritual level rather than in a social hierarchy. It is a way of avoiding seeking perfection in others, even as we perfect ourselves in spite of the things that shame us.

This attitude cultivates humility and the courage to persevere beyond the suffering inflicted on us by others who may hinder our motivation to live a more fulfilling life. In this regard, the most profound form of revenge is to persevere despite the obstacles placed in our path and the determination of others to suppress the expression of our spiritual authenticity. While it makes sense to associate our accomplishments with the challenges posed by those who have attempted to impede our progress, the relevance of the impact of their actions is only relative to our determination to succeed.

Social authority, a representation of the karma that people we encounter on our spiritual path have brought upon themselves by seeking social validation, is the same karma we come with when we are born into a reality that is designed to suppress spiritual authenticity. It is here, on earth, that we find the real battle between evil, represented by authority, and good, associated with our divine spark that drives us forward to manifest a better life, fueled by a sense of spiritual fulfillment.

In summary, our deepest desires are inextricably linked to our soul's purpose, and suffering can catalyze dreams of our true destiny. Karma, like a cosmic teacher, gently nudges us toward salvation through forgiveness and spiritual growth.

Chapter 16: Cultivating Self-Confidence Through Self-Reliance

When we fail to recognize the negative influences of our upbringing and our tendency to blindly obey authority figures, we ultimately fail ourselves. Seeking to understand the world and our place in it fosters confidence and empowers self-reliance. But beyond knowledge and wisdom, we must learn to discern the difference between beliefs that empower us and those that hold us back.

Loving ourselves, being wise, and setting clear boundaries helps us to surround ourselves with supportive people who encourage and empower us as we grow and become more self-reliant. Self-reliance is the foundation of unwavering trust. While envy and competition can cause others to resort to deception and hinder our progress, spiritual evolution requires breaking negative karmic cycles. This can be accomplished through self-forgiveness and personal growth. To foster feelings of adequacy, competence, and confidence, it's important to develop habits that fill us with these emotions.

Sometimes taking up a hobby or playing a video game can be beneficial. Engaging in hobbies and video games has been linked to positive effects on mental health and well-being. For example, a study by Granic, Lobel, and Engels (2014) found that video games can fulfill basic psychological needs such as competence, autonomy, and relatedness. The study suggests that video games can provide a sense of accomplishment, which is essential for overall happiness and mental health.

Moreover, in the pursuit of personal growth and fulfillment, few tools are as powerful as the art of visualization. By harnessing the immense potential of our minds, we can transcend the limitations of our current circumstances and create our own destiny. Our thoughts and beliefs shape our reality, and the mental images we hold significantly influence our actions, emotions, and ultimately the results we experience. When we vividly visualize ourselves achieving our goals, we activate neural pathways that prepare our brains for success.

Visualization not only increases our confidence and motivation, it also helps us identify and overcome potential obstacles. By creating a clear and detailed mental picture of our goals, we tap into our subconscious' innate creativity and problem-solving abilities. This process allows us to anticipate challenges, develop effective strategies, and cultivate the skills and resources necessary to turn our dreams into reality.

To fully harness the power of visualization, approach it with intention and consistency. Set aside a few minutes each day to vividly visualize your goals, including sensory details and emotional experiences. Experiment with different techniques, such as creating a vision board, writing detailed descriptions of your desired future, or engaging in guided meditations, to discover what works best for you. With unwavering commitment and a deep understanding of your motivational landscape, you can manifest the vision of what you've always wanted.

When used collectively, this powerful tool can catalyze positive change on a societal level. By encouraging others to visualize a more just, equitable, and sustainable world, we can inspire collective action and foster the awareness needed to address pressing challenges. Imagine a world where leaders, policymakers, and citizens use visualization to envision a future of peace, prosperity, and environmental stewardship.

By aligning our individual and collective visions, we can harness the synergistic potential of our shared aspirations to overcome even the most formidable obstacles. However, this requires navigating the tension between the desires of our souls and the rationalizations of our egos. The ego, driven by fear and self-preservation, clings to the familiar and resists change, while the soul yearns to grow and pushes us toward our highest potential. Recognizing and transcending the manipulative tactics of the ego, such as self-doubt and the lure of instant gratification, is crucial to unlocking our true power. A fixed mindset perceives talents as innate and unchangeable, but by reframing negative thoughts, practicing gratitude, and visualizing success, we can cultivate a more constructive and empowering mental framework.

In summary, self-reliance, fostered by self-love, wisdom, and setting boundaries, is critical to building confidence and breaking negative karmic cycles. Engaging in hobbies, practicing visualization, and cultivating positive mental habits can help us achieve our goals and manifest our desires. In addition, collective visualization has the power to inspire social change, leading to a more just, equitable, and sustainable world.

Chapter 17: Emotional Mastery and the Pursuit of Dreams

Our understanding and interpretation of the world is inherently subjective, as we filter information through our existing knowledge structures and emotional patterns shaped by past experiences. By recognizing this complexity and actively seeking to understand diverse perspectives, we approach life's challenges with greater empathy and discernment. Embracing the unknown with an open mind and a passion for learning opens doors to new dimensions of personal growth.

The mind and heart are inextricably linked and influence each other; therefore, by learning to understand and regulate our emotions, we gain the power to make choices that align with our core values and long-term aspirations. Accurately identifying and labeling our emotions is a critical step toward emotional mastery. In addition, by exploring our emotional landscape, we develop greater resilience and cultivate more meaningful connections with others. This leads to increased productivity as we focus our energy on what really matters.

Emotional mastery also enhances our ability to manage stress and prevent burnout. Recognizing and addressing our emotional needs reduces feelings of overwhelm and maintains the balance and well-being essential for sustained high performance. Central to this framework is the importance of establishing daily habits and routines that support our overall well-being. These seemingly insignificant actions, such as regular exercise, mindful eating, and consistent meditation, lay the foundation for success in all other aspects of life.

When we manage our emotions with awareness and compassion, we tap into resilience and creativity. In a world that often values logic and rationality over emotional intelligence, cultivating emotional mastery serves as a powerful counterbalance. By aligning the wisdom of our hearts with the clarity of our minds, we unlock a deeper understanding for better decision-making.

Emotions can be managed through intentional actions, which are ultimately influenced by our beliefs. By consciously choosing a positive mindset fueled by optimism, we can create opportunities for happiness and success. This deterministic influence shapes our experiences and leads to higher consciousness. Despite the barriers to understanding we may encounter along the way, the humility to acknowledge these limitations allows us to approach the unknown with wonder and openness, rather than clinging to preconceived notions that may hinder our growth.

This humility is essential to the realization of our dreams, for dreams, when combined with intense emotional experiences, possess an inherent energy that transcends the limits of logical thought. Dreams aren't just passive reflections of our subconscious, but rather catalysts for transformative change. Dreams fueled by passion and emotional intensity can serve as powerful conduits for self-actualization, pushing us beyond our comfort zones and revealing new dimensions of our existence that were previously hidden from our awareness.

Embracing the transformative power of our dreams allows us to explore deeper into our consciousness and perceive existence on multiple levels. In this realm, the tangible world of physical matter becomes a subjective interpretation of a greater spiritual reality. As we transcend into the unknown, we encounter a more vivid manifestation of both the benevolent and malevolent forces that shape our lives and challenge us to confront the complexities of our existence with heightened awareness. And this heightened awareness allows us to transcend the limitations of time and space and perceive the interconnectedness of all things.

For those who embrace this perspective, the distinctions between past, present, and future become blurred, and the constructs that guide our existence become portals to new realms of understanding. By perceiving time as a fluid continuum rather than a rigid sequence, we can unlock insights that were previously inaccessible. This shift in perception encourages us to see our experiences not as isolated events, but as interconnected threads woven into the fabric of our lives. This interconnectedness fosters a sense of unity and purpose, allowing us to see the larger patterns that influence our journey. As we begin to recognize these patterns, we gain the ability to navigate life's complexities with greater ease and insight.

In summary, emotional mastery, achieved through self-awareness and intentional action, is critical to personal growth and success. By aligning emotions with values and dreams, we can unleash creativity, resilience, and a deeper understanding of the world. This heightened awareness transcends time and space, revealing the interconnectedness and unity of all things.

Chapter 18: Overcoming Ego and Embracing Truth

Every aspect of our lives is a reflection of our inner self. The external world we perceive is not a fixed reality, but a composite of collective agreements, thoughts and beliefs. Therefore, lasting change requires a deep commitment to personal transformation. Embracing the unknown and the potential of a hypothetical future is a critical part of this transformative process. Many successful companies have emerged from setbacks with opportunities overlooked by others precisely because the individuals in leadership positions dared to take unconventional paths and challenge conventional wisdom.

However, the human mind, often limited by its linear perception of time and sequence, struggles to fully comprehend the multidimensional nature of reality. This limitation can lead to a narrow perspective that traps individuals in a cycle of complacency and prevents them from realizing their true potential. Overcoming this limitation requires a fundamental shift in mindset, from viewing the world through a lens of scarcity to embracing an abundance mindset.

Instead of being paralyzed by self-doubt and the belief that resources are finite, we must recognize the limitless potential within ourselves and the universe that inspires us to courageous and inspired action. We must be open to letting go of outdated ways of thinking and embracing new perspectives as we let go of the limitations of the past and embrace the limitless potential of the present moment.

In the face of uncertainty, we discover opportunities for evolution and the realization of our full potential. By confronting our fears, insecurities, and shadows, we unlock the keys to personal transformation. It is in the crucible of discomfort that we build the resilience and clarity to transcend our limitations. Furthermore, as our understanding of life's purpose expands, our questions lose their meaning. Embracing the mystery and grandeur of existence reveals the true freedom to create, love, and live authentically.

This attitude goes beyond a positive outlook; it's a profound belief in the inherent benevolence of the universe and the divine orchestration of our dreams and aspirations. It embodies the realization that because our existence transcends the physical realm and continues its journey beyond this world, we are not mere products of our circumstances, but vessels for the divine spark that animates the universe.

Ignorance of historical and transcendent truths is no excuse for shirking our spiritual responsibilities. Historical events demonstrate that humanity often confronts its deepest fears despite attempts to ignore or repress them. The silence of many about these cycles only perpetuates misunderstanding and conflict. True blindness is a state in which individuals cannot see beyond their deeply held beliefs and assumptions.

This limited perception hinders spiritual growth and traps people in cycles of ignorance and repeating the same mistakes. In fact, many people tend to become so overly attached to their egos that they disregard the truth and secretly wish for the failure, misfortune, or even death of those they ostracize in order to validate themselves. This very common ego-driven mindset creates an environment that hinders spiritual authenticity and progress on our planet.

We can see this all around us, for communicating deeper truths to someone who is fixated on personal beliefs and dogmas can be challenging, as they may reject or undermine the efforts of those trying to enlighten them. Such people rarely change, and if forced to coexist with someone wiser, they may resort to slander and attempt to banish that person from their environment. This may involve extreme measures such as imprisonment or even murder. Such resistance to growth and change often stems from deep-seated fear and insecurity. But despite the many interests at play, destiny is a matter of self-determination, and there is no karma without consent and purpose. Thus, the pursuit of our dreams requires not only a vision and the knowledge of how to achieve it, but also the courage to act on it.

Only fools, driven by ignorance, typically draw unrealistic conclusions from what they don't understand in order to justify their state of existence. Wisdom lies in humility and recognizing one's limitations without succumbing to them. Unseen truths remain elusive unless we expand our consciousness. However, education can sometimes mislead us into believing false truths, leading our minds astray into chaos. For this reason, many cling to false survival patterns that are far from the truth, and these deeply ingrained and often unquestioned patterns hinder true growth and understanding.

In summary, personal transformation involves cultivating an abundance mindset, facing our fears head-on, and discarding outdated beliefs that no longer serve us. By expanding our consciousness and seeking truth beyond societal norms, we can break free from limiting patterns and embrace our authentic selves and our true purpose.

Chapter 19: The Universal Purpose

We are all part of the same universal purpose, moving toward it in different ways. This purpose thrives on positive and loving emotions and ultimately leads us to enlightenment through self-knowledge and the responsible actions we take along the way. Although we are constantly searching for this truth without ever fully grasping it, if this truth were within us, our dilemmas would seem like mere illusions. Therefore, it is wiser to focus on our goals without fixating on how to achieve them. Remarkable achievements in life often come unexpectedly and defy conventional logic.

We often cling to what we perceive as ours and define ourselves by it, but judging ourselves and others based on our assumptions - rooted in primitive instincts and shaped by past experiences - limits our potential as human beings and diminishes the potential value of our life experiences. When illusions are exposed, the immature and dogmatic mind often resorts to skepticism. Just as love seems unreal to those who have never experienced it, trust has no meaning to those who have only known betrayal, and the light of truth fails to enchant those who are entranced by the darkness of their inner thoughts.

For many, comforting self-deception is all they have, and the meaning they attach to it is all they can comprehend. People exist at different levels of consciousness that manifest in their actions, thoughts, speech, emotions, reactions, and desires, but to grow beyond a certain spiritual level, we must make a commitment to study, develop, apply, and achieve tangible results that expand our awareness of life. Especially in difficult times, it's crucial to intensify your efforts to study and work diligently.

Although many people believe they have a complete understanding of reality, a deeper investigation reveals beliefs rooted in the ego and collective illusions formed by shared beliefs and perceptions that go unchallenged. This collective illusion is not objective unless it's universally accepted and agreed upon. It does not stand the test of time. Yet a collective lie can indeed sustain a time-bound reality that defies logic and common sense, as we've seen throughout human history.

The deepest secret hidden from the public is also the most obvious: beliefs shape our reality. When we fail to consciously act on our beliefs, we succumb to the reality of others. When people refuse to acknowledge the reality imposed on them and instead seek deeper meaning in collective delusions, they rely on luck for their outcomes and expect things to happen by chance. They surrender completely to the reality imposed upon them, confusing it with a divine order.

In the midst of these individuals, the true brilliance of a successful person shines through in their approach to life. What some perceive as genius or luck is simply the culmination of persistent effort and deep reflection beyond conventional wisdom. The dedication to in-depth research and learning is what separates some from others. By recognizing the cyclical nature of the human experience and the importance of humility, they transcend limited perceptions and contribute to the collective evolution of humanity. But through unwavering commitment, introspection, and the courage to challenge conventional norms, we too can create lives of purpose and lasting impact.

By cultivating a higher consciousness and questioning the assumptions we've accepted as truths, we open ourselves to unpredictable outcomes. Doubt and uncertainty may arise along the way, but by persevering, we build the resilience and strength to overcome obstacles and achieve our goals. To break free from negative cycles, however, we must acknowledge the limitations and imperfections of ourselves and others. Forgiveness, confidence, and emotional mastery can propel us forward and help us overcome obstacles that once seemed insurmountable.

By confronting negative thought patterns and taking decisive action, we can gradually silence self-doubt and cultivate self-belief. This commitment to learning, coupled with humility, empowers us to overcome limitations and achieve success in all areas of life.

In summary, humanity is on a path to enlightenment, guided by a universal purpose that demands self-knowledge and responsible action. While some cling to self-deception and collective illusion, others transcend these limitations and embrace a higher consciousness. By challenging societal norms and dedicating themselves to introspection, these individuals break free from negative cycles and achieve a higher consciousness that leads them to remarkable success. These are the people humanity needs to evolve to the highest levels, limited only by imagination.

Chapter 20: Mastering the Art of Getting Things Done

The following 10 key principles summarize the teachings on overcoming procrastination. By incorporating them into your daily life, you can greatly increase your productivity and achieve your goals more effectively.

1. Align your actions with your core values: True motivation comes from living in alignment with your core values and dreams. When your goals align with your beliefs, you'll naturally have the drive to achieve them.

2. Embrace autonomy and mastery: Cultivating a sense of autonomy and control over your life is critical. Autonomy drives motivation, while mastery involves the continuous process of growth and learning. Together, they create a powerful force for personal development.

3. Break tasks into manageable steps: Large tasks can feel overwhelming and lead to procrastination. By breaking them down into smaller, achievable steps, you can build momentum and make progress feel more attainable.

4. Create a supportive environment: Surround yourself with supportive people and create a distraction-free workspace. A conducive environment increases focus and motivation, setting the stage for success.

5. Use deadlines effectively: Instead of viewing deadlines as stressors, use them to create urgency and prioritize tasks. Deadlines can be powerful motivators when approached with the right mindset.

6. Control your emotions: Emotional regulation is key to productivity. It helps you make smart decisions and stay motivated, even in challenging situations.

7. Challenge negative self-talk: Procrastination is often caused by self-doubt and negative thoughts. Actively challenge these thoughts and replace them with affirmations of your strengths and abilities to build confidence.

8. Celebrate small victories: Acknowledge and celebrate small victories along the way. This builds confidence and reinforces positive behavior, creating a reward loop that encourages further action.

9. Use visualization: Visualization involves mentally rehearsing desired outcomes and the steps needed to achieve them. This

powerful technique can increase motivation and set you up for success by preparing your mind for the tasks ahead.

10. Forgive and move on: Practice self-forgiveness and accept that you and others are imperfect. By freeing yourself from negative thought patterns and cycles, you can unlock your full potential and grow as an individual.

In addition to these principles, the book emphasizes a comprehensive set of skills that, when developed and practiced, can significantly increase productivity and help overcome procrastination:

Introspection: Understanding personal motivations, triggers, and patterns of procrastination.

Regulation: Effectively managing emotions to maintain motivation, productivity, and resilience.

Planning: Setting clear, specific, achievable, relevant, and time-bound goals to provide direction and purpose.

Prioritizing: Implementing productivity techniques and tools to improve time management and focus on high-priority tasks.

Discipline: Cultivating consistent habits and routines that support long-term goals and promote self-control.

Visualization: Mentally rehearsing desired outcomes and the steps required to achieve them to increase motivation and preparedness.

Flexibility: Learning from setbacks and adjusting strategies as needed to overcome challenges.

Optimism: Maintaining a positive attitude, practicing self-compassion, and reframing negative thoughts to maintain a positive outlook.

Communication: Developing and maintaining supportive relationships that provide motivation, accountability, and encouragement.

Focus: Engaging in present-moment awareness and reflection to increase focus, clarity, and emotional well-being.

By mastering these principles and skills, you'll be well equipped to overcome procrastination and achieve your goals with greater efficiency and satisfaction.

Chapter 21: 10 Daily Questions for Motivation and Discipline

Here are ten daily questions to help you stay motivated, disciplined, and free from procrastination based on the principles in this book:

1. Are my current actions aligned with my core values and long-term goals? Reflecting on this question ensures that your daily activities are aligned with what is truly important to you, which fosters intrinsic motivation.

2. Am I taking steps today to cultivate my sense of autonomy and mastery? Consider whether you're engaging in empowering activities that promote personal growth, which is essential for maintaining motivation.

3. Have I broken down my tasks into manageable steps? Assess whether you've broken down larger projects into smaller,

actionable tasks to avoid feeling overwhelmed and build momentum.

4. Is my environment supportive and productive? Evaluate whether your environment, including the people you interact with, helps or hinders your focus and motivation.

5. Do I use deadlines effectively to create urgency and prioritize my tasks? Reflect on how you perceive deadlines - are they stressors or motivators? Adjust your mindset accordingly.

6. How am I managing my emotions today? Consider whether you're in control of your emotional reactions and whether they're helping or hindering your productivity.

7. What negative self-talk am I experiencing and how can I challenge it? Identify any self-doubt or negative thoughts and actively replace them with affirmations that reinforce your strengths.

8. Did I celebrate any small victories today? Acknowledge your accomplishments, no matter how small, to build confidence and create a positive feedback loop that encourages further action.

9. Do I use visualization techniques to prepare for my tasks? Consider whether you're mentally rehearsing your desired results and the steps needed to achieve them, which can increase motivation.

10. Did I practice self-forgiveness today? Consider whether you're letting go of past mistakes and imperfections, which is essential for personal growth and reaching your full potential.

Asking yourself these questions regularly can help you stay focused on your goals, increase your productivity, and effectively overcome procrastination. This practice encourages self-reflection and proactive changes to your daily habits, ultimately leading to greater success and fulfillment in both your personal and professional life.

Glossary of Terms

Anticipation: It serves as a powerful motivator and performance enhancer, similar to having a mental roadmap that ensures we complete tasks effectively.

Deadlines: They act as time-bound constraints that provide focus and maintain progress. They create a sense of urgency and guide us in prioritizing tasks.

Emotional mastery: This involves understanding and managing our emotions. It facilitates informed decision-making, increases productivity, and contributes to overall well-being.

Gamification: This approach turns ordinary tasks into engaging games, using rewards and challenges to maintain motivation and engagement.

Growth mindset: The belief that skills can be developed through hard work and dedication. It serves as a powerful tool for overcoming obstacles and achieving goals.

Imposter Syndrome: This phenomenon occurs when individuals experience a sense of inadequacy despite evidence of their skills and abilities.

Micro-steps: These are small, consistent actions that build momentum and reduce the overwhelming feeling associated with large tasks.

Momentum: Similar to a boulder rolling downhill, it propels the individual forward with each successive, purposeful action.

Motivation: It drives individuals to take action and complete tasks. It is derived from a variety of factors, including personal values, goals, emotional states, and external influences. Understanding and aligning actions with these motivational drivers is critical to overcoming procrastination and achieving goals.

Procrastination: Procrastination is the act of putting off or avoiding a task or responsibility. It often results from a lack of motivation, self-control, or effective time management. To effectively combat procrastination, it is important to identify and address its underlying causes.

Purposeful Productivity: Purposeful productivity involves completing daily tasks and habits in a way that aligns with one's values and goals. This sense of purpose provides the motivation to persevere and fosters a sense of fulfillment.

Reward Loop: The reward loop is a pattern of behavior that shapes our actions. Positive reinforcement, such as rewards, encourages us to repeat those behaviors. This principle underlies the effectiveness of gamification and other motivational strategies.

Self-Control: Self-control is the ability to regulate impulses, emotions, and behaviors. It serves as the foundation for personal growth and goal achievement.

Visualization: Visualization is the mental imagery and rehearsal of desired outcomes. It helps develop skills by creating a mental representation of success. Visualization is a powerful tool for overcoming procrastination and achieving goals.

References

Aafjes-Doorn, K., Garay, C., Etchebarne, I., Kamsteeg, C., & Rousso, A. (2020). Psychotherapy for personal growth: A multicultural and multitheoretical exploration. *Journal of Clinical Psychology*.

Abdel-Khalik, A., Adam, S., & Azeem, H. A. (2021). Developing strategies for overcoming challenges faced by postgraduate nursing students. *Journal of Advanced Nursing, 77*(12), 737–750.

Adrianson, L., Ancok, D., Ramdhani, N., & Archer, T. (2013). Cultural influences upon health, affect, self-esteem and impulsiveness: An Indonesian-Swedish comparison. *International Journal of Research Studies in Psychology, 2*(2), 25–44.

Al-Mansoori, R. S., Al-Thani, D., & Ali, R. (2023). Designing for digital wellbeing: From theory to practice a scoping review. *Human Behavior and Emerging Technologies*.

Aschieri, F., Emmerik, A. V., Wibbelink, C. J. M., & Kamphuis, J. (2023). A systematic research review of collaborative assessment methods. *Psychotherapy*.

Bandyopadhyay, N. (2016). The role of self-esteem, negative affect and normative influence in impulse buying. *Marketing Intelligence & Planning, 34*(4), 523–539.

Basabe, N., Harizmendi, M., Carrasco, J. J. P., Telletxea, S., Castro-Abril, P., & Padoan, S. (2021). Collective violence and construction of peace culture in the Basque Country: Two experiences of memory, recognition and forgiveness. *Deusto Journal of Human Rights.*

Bast, D., & Barnes-Holmes, D. (2015a). Priming thoughts of failing versus succeeding and performance on the implicit relational assessment procedure (IRAP) as a measure of self-forgiveness. *The Psychological Record, 65*(4), 667–678.

Bast, D., & Barnes-Holmes, D. (2015b). Priming thoughts of failing versus succeeding and performance on the implicit relational assessment procedure (IRAP) as a measure of self-forgiveness. *The Psychological Record, 65*(4), 667–678.

Bernal-Guerrero, A., Cárdenas-Gutiérrez, A. R., & Martín-Gutiérrez, Á. (2023). Systemic approach to entrepreneurial identity and its educational projection. *Philosophies.*

Blom, V., Richter, A., Hallsten, L., & Svedberg, P. (2015). The associations between job insecurity, depressive symptoms and burnout: The role of performance-based self-esteem. *Economic and Industrial Democracy, 39*(1), 48–63.

Brown, J. D. (2010). High self-esteem buffers negative feedback: Once more with feeling. *Cognition and Emotion, 24*(8), 1389–1404.

Bryngeirsdottir, H. S., & Halldórsdóttir, S. (2022a). Fourteen main obstacles on the journey to post-traumatic growth as experienced by female survivors of intimate partner violence: "It was all so confusing." *International Journal of Environmental Research and Public Health, 19*(1).

Bryngeirsdottir, H. S., & Halldórsdóttir, S. (2022b). "I'm a winner, not a victim": The facilitating factors of post-traumatic growth among women who have suffered intimate partner violence. *International Journal of Environmental Research and Public Health, 19*(1).

Buitrago, M. F., Jara, L. M. M., Pérez, N. D. V., & García, N. G. (2023). Adaptation strategies in students with motor functional diversity. *Investigación y Educación En Enfermería, 41*(1).

Burton, J. P., Mitchell, T., & Lee, T. W. (2005). The role of self-esteem and social influences in aggressive reactions to interactional injustice. *Journal of Business and Psychology, 20*(2), 131–170.

Calvo, V., & Bianco, F. (2015). Influence of adult attachment insecurities on parenting self-esteem: The mediating role of dyadic adjustment. *Frontiers in Psychology, 6.*

Cameron, J. J., Stinson, D. A., Hoplock, L., Hole, C., & Schellenberg, J. (2016). The robust self-esteem proxy: Impressions of self-esteem inform judgments of personality and social value. *Self and Identity, 15*(5), 561–578.

Cavallo, J. V., & Hirniak, A. (2019). No assistance desired: How perceptions of others' self-esteem affect support-seeking. *Social Psychological and Personality Science, 10*(2), 193–200.

Chavez, F. L. C., Wolford, S. N., Kimmes, J. G., May, R., & Fincham, F. (2019). "I had let everyone, including myself, down": Illuminating the self-forgiveness process among female college students. *Journal of College and Character, 20*(2), 123–143.

Ćirjaković, D. S. (2024). Words that heal – Bibliotherapy for children's emotional and social growth. *Detinjstvo*.

Cowden, R., & Worthington, E. (2019). Overcoming failure in sport: A self-forgiveness framework. *Journal of Human Sport and Exercise*.

Cunff, A.-L. L. (2019). Mindframing: A proposed framework for personal growth.

DeMarco, M. J. (2024). 6-Fold path to self-forgiveness: An interdisciplinary model for the treatment of moral injury with intervention strategies for clinicians. *Frontiers in Psychology, 15*.

Duru, E., Balkıs, M., & Duru, S. (2023). Procrastination among adults: The role of self-doubt, fear of the negative evaluation, and irrational/rational beliefs. *Journal of Evidence-Based Psychotherapies*.

Erzar, T. (2018). Self-perceived victimhood and forgiveness in different generations of the right and left political group in Slovenia.

Gál, É., Tóth-Király, I., Szamosközi, I., & Orosz, G. (2020). Fixed intelligence mindset moderates the impact of adverse academic experiences on students' self-esteem. *Journal of College Student Retention, 24*(6), 1028–1053.

Gao, Y. (2024). Comparison of compulsory education between China and Britain. *Lecture Notes in Education Psychology and Public Media.*

Geraci, A. (2023). Teachers' emotional intelligence, burnout, work engagement, and self-efficacy during COVID-19 lockdown. *Behavioral Science, 13.*

Gilbert, P., & Woodyatt, L. (2017). An evolutionary approach to shame-based self-criticism, self-forgiveness, and compassion. In *The handbook of self-enhancement and self-protection* (pp. 29–41). Guilford Press.

Gilbey, D., Perry, Y., Lin, A., & Ohan, J. (2022). "Shame, doubt and sadness": A qualitative investigation of the experience of self-stigma in adolescents with diverse sexual orientations. *Youth.*

Gold, R., & Gold, A. (2023). "Am I a good enough therapist": Self-doubt among speech and language therapists. *International Journal of Language and Communication Disorders.*

Goodwyn, A. (2018). From personal growth (1966) to personal growth and social agency (2016) – proposing an invigorated model for the 21st century. *The Future of English Teaching Worldwide.*

Han, K. (2023). The role of the prison library. International Journal of Education and Humanities.

Hindmarch, L. (2008). An exploration of the experience of self-doubt in the coaching context and the strategies adopted by coaches to overcome it. *International Journal of Evidence Based Coaching and Mentoring, 6*(2), 1–13.

Hlava, P., Elfers, J., Bieber, J., Maitra, S., Burge, C., Howard, A., Carbajal, R., Jamieson, M., & Casey, A. (2024). Reorienting through the body: The correlation among self-transcendent emotion experiences and interoceptive awareness. *Journal of Humanistic Psychology.*

Ilies, R., Pater, I. D., & Judge, T. (2007). Differential affective reactions to negative and positive feedback, and the role of self-esteem. *Journal of Managerial Psychology, 22*(6), 590–609.

Kaygusuz, R., Tolan, Ö. Ç., & Aydoğdu, B. E. (2023). Mediating role of self-reflection and insight in the relationship between forgiveness and Gestalt contact disturbances. *Anadolu Üniversitesi Eğitim Fakültesi Dergisi.*

Kielkiewicz, K., Mathúna, C. Ó., & McLaughlin, C. (2019). Construct validity and dimensionality of the Rosenberg self-esteem scale and its association with spiritual values within Irish population. *Journal of Religion and Health, 59*(3), 381–398.

Kim, H. K. (2014). Overcoming resistance to health persuasion: Strategies to reduce self-defense motives.

Kita, Y., & Inoue, Y. (2017). The direct/indirect association of ADHD/ODD symptoms with self-esteem, self-perception, and depression in early adolescents. *Frontiers in Psychiatry, 8.*

Kocollari, U., Cavicchioli, M., & Demaria, F. (2023). The 5 E(lements) of employee-centric corporate social responsibility and their stimulus on happiness at work: An empirical investigation. *Corporate Social Responsibility and Environmental Management.*

Kolbina, L., Kasianenko, O., Sopivnyk, I., Karskanova, S., & Chepka, O. (2023). The role of inclusive education in the personal growth of a child with special educational needs. *Revista Amazonía Investiga.*

Kostromina, S., & Makarova, M. (2023). Quasi-development as an illusion of personal growth. *Changing Societies & Personalities.*

Lee, E., Choi, T. R., & Lee, T. (2023). The mediating role of forgiveness and self-efficacy in the relationship between childhood maltreatment and treatment motivation among Malaysian male drug addicts. *Frontiers in Psychology, 13.*

Miranti, M., & Karmiyati, D. (2024). Strategies for overcoming Cinderella complex syndrome in adolescent girls. *Vitamin: Jurnal Ilmu Kesehatan Umum.*

Mróz, J., Toussaint, L. L., & Kaleta, K. (2024). Association between religiosity and forgiveness: Testing a moderated mediation model of self-compassion and adverse childhood experiences. *Religions.*

Neiss, M. B., Stevenson, J., Legrand, L., Iacono, W., & Sedikides, C. (2009). Self-esteem, negative emotionality, and depression as a common temperamental core: A study of mid-adolescent twin girls. *Journal of Personality, 77*(2), 327–346.

Neiss, M. B., Stevenson, J., Sedikides, C., Kumashiro, M., Finkel, E., & Rusbult, C. (2005). Executive self, self-esteem, and negative affectivity: Relations at the phenotypic and genotypic level.

Nyuiemedi, A. E.-T., & Richardson, A.-M. (2024). Surviving child labour through forgiveness and self-efficacy: Implications for counselling practice. *International Journal of Psychology and Counselling.*

Oktriani, D. R., Hufad, A., & Utami, N. (2023). Overcoming the character crisis in children: Strategies, outcomes, and evaluations of Bina desa program. *Utamax Journal of Ultimate Research and Trends in Education.*

Oliveira, W., Esteca, A. M. N. N., Wechsler, S. M., & Menesini, E. (2024). Bullying and cyberbullying in school: Rapid review on the roles of gratitude, forgiveness, and self-regulation. *International Journal of Environmental Research and Public Health, 21*(1).

Onal, A. A., & Yalçin, I. (2017). Self-forgiveness: The predictive role of cognitive distortions.

Paleari, G. F., Danioni, F., Pelucchi, S., Lombrano, M. R., Lumera, D., & Regalia, C. (2022). The relationship between self-forgiveness and psychological wellbeing in prison inmates: The mediating role of mindfulness. *Criminal Behaviour and Mental Health, 32*(4), 337–349.

Paluckaitė, U., & Žardeckaitė-Matulaitienė, K. (2019). Overcoming strategies of adolescents' risky online self-disclosure. *E-Methodology.*

Park, H.-J., & Jeon, K. (2013). Fashion savvy II: The influences of fear of negative evaluation by others, self-esteem, and consumer confidence in fashion decisions on fashion savvy. *The Research Journal of the Costume Culture, 21*(4), 562–575.

Perikova, E., & Bysova, V. M. (2018). Metacognition strategies in overcoming difficult life situations with the main focus on different levels of personal self-regulation. *The Novosibirsk State Pedagogical University Bulletin.*

Ponomarenko, N. (2022). Different approaches to the definition of the concept of "need for self-realization" in professional activity. *Educational Dimension.*

Ponte, J. P. M. D., Quaresma, M., & Mata-Pereira, J. (2022). Teachers' learning in lesson study: Insights provided by a modified version of the interconnected model of teacher professional growth. *ZDM – Mathematics Education, 54*(3), 373–386.

Purebl, G., Schnitzspahn, K., & Zsák, É. (2023). Overcoming treatment gaps in the management of depression with non-pharmacological adjunctive strategies. *Frontiers in Psychiatry, 14.*

Reitzes, D., Mutran, E., & Fernandez, M. E. (1996). Preretirement influences on postretirement self-esteem. *The Journals of Gerontology Series B: Psychological Sciences and Social Sciences, 51*(5), S242-9.

Ricciardelli, L., & McCabe, M. (2001). Self-esteem and negative affect as moderators of sociocultural influences on body dissatisfaction, strategies to decrease weight, and strategies to increase muscles among adolescent boys and girls. *Sex Roles, 44*(3-4), 189–207.

Rose, A. D. (1995). The dynamics of personal growth, development and change. *Adult Learning, 6*(3), 29–5.

Ruini, C., Offidani, E., & Vescovelli, F. (2015). Life stressors, allostatic overload, and their impact on posttraumatic growth. *Journal of Loss and Trauma, 20*(2), 109–122.

Sica, L., & Sestito, L. A. (2021). Personal skills for optimal identity development: A person-centered approach in Italian late-adolescents. *Journal for Person-Oriented Research, 7*(1), 36–51.

Silverberg, C. M. (2019). Critical embodied praxis for social justice and peace educators: A story of personal transformation through analysis of my Jewish and settler identities.

Skolnick, V. G., Lynch, B., Smith, L., Romanowicz, M., Blain, G., & Toussaint, L. (2023). The association between parent and child ACEs is buffered by forgiveness of others and self-forgiveness. *Journal of Child and Adolescent Trauma, 16*(4), 995–1003.

Suh, A., & Cheung, C. M. K. (2017). Beyond hedonic enjoyment: Conceptualizing eudaimonic motivation for personal informatics technology usage. *Interacción, 119–133.*

Swiger, T. (2020). Morally injurious experiences of combat-exposed veterans of Iraq and Afghanistan: Moderating effects of self-forgiveness on feelings of shame and guilt.

Thompson, J. K., Shroff, H., Herbozo, S., Cafri, G., Rodriguez, J., & Rodriguez, M. (2007). Relations among multiple peer influences, body dissatisfaction, eating disturbance, and self-esteem: A comparison of average weight, at risk of overweight, and overweight adolescent girls. *Journal of Pediatric Psychology, 32*(1), 24–29.

Tyan, M. (2023). The influence of the main strategies overcoming stress on professional activity of transport police officers. *Applied Psychology and Pedagogy.*

Tyler, J., Branch, S., & Kearns, P. (2016). Dispositional need to belong moderates the impact of negative social cues and rejection on self-esteem. *Social Psychology, 47*(2), 179–186.

Vets, I. V. (2023). Conscious self-regulation and coping strategies as resources for overcoming difficult life situations. *Theoretical and Experimental Psychology.*

Walbrugh, V. (2016). How to deal with low self-esteem: A 5-step, CBT-based plan for overcoming thoughts and eliminating self-doubt. *Educational Psychology in Practice, 32*(3), 324–324.

Westover, J. (2024). Overcoming feelings of being stuck: Strategies for moving your career forward. *Human Capital Leadership Review*.

Woodyatt, L., Cornish, M., & Cibich, M. (2017). Self-forgiveness at work: Finding pathways to renewal when coping with failure or perceived transgressions. In *The handbook of self-enhancement and self-protection* (pp. 293–307). Guilford Press.

Wu, J., Cheung, H., & Chan, R. (2017). Changing definition of teacher professionalism: Autonomy and accountability. In *Educational governance and accountability* (pp. 59–70). Springer.

Wu, L.-Z., Birtch, T. A., Chiang, F., & Zhang, H. (2018). Perceptions of negative workplace gossip: A self-consistency theory framework. *Journal of Management, 44*(5), 1873–1898.

Yashchenko, E. (2023). Interpersonal conflict, values, strategies for overcoming stress situations of students before and after the start of a special military operation. *Вестник Университета*.

Zaki, A., Nasution, I., Informasi, L., lDiri, K., & Smartphone, K. (2023). Implementation of information services through self-control strategies in overcoming smartphone addiction in students. *Jurnal Ilmiah Sekolah Dasar*.

Book Review Request

Dear reader,

Thank you for purchasing this book! I would love to know your opinion. Writing a book review helps in understanding the readers and also impacts other readers' purchasing decisions. Your opinion matters. Please write a book review!

Your kindness is greatly appreciated!

About the Author

Dan Desmarques is a renowned author with a remarkable track record in the literary world. With an impressive portfolio of 28 Amazon bestsellers, including eight #1 bestsellers, Dan is a respected figure in the industry. Drawing on his background as a college professor of academic and creative writing, as well as his experience as a seasoned business consultant, Dan brings a unique blend of expertise to his work. His profound insights and transformational content appeal to a wide audience, covering topics as diverse as personal growth, success, spirituality, and the deeper meaning of life. Through his writing, Dan empowers readers to break free from limitations, unlock their inner potential, and embark on a journey of self-discovery and transformation. In a competitive self-help market, Dan's exceptional talent and inspiring stories make him a standout author, motivating readers to engage with his books and embark on a path of personal growth and enlightenment.

Also Written by the Author

1. 66 Days to Change Your Life: 12 Steps to Effortlessly Remove Mental Blocks, Reprogram Your Brain and Become a Money Magnet

2. A New Way of Being: How to Rewire Your Brain and Take Control of Your Life

3. Abnormal: How to Train Yourself to Think Differently and Permanently Overcome Evil Thoughts

4. Alignment: The Process of Transmutation Within the Mechanics of Life

5. Audacity: How to Make Fast and Efficient Decisions in Any Situation

6. Beyond Belief: Discovering Sacred Moments in Everyday Life

7. Beyond Illusions: Discovering Your True Nature

About the Publisher

This book was published by 22 Lions Publishing.

www.22Lions.com